GILLS AND BILLS

Martha K. Resnick

Carolyn J. Hyatt

STECK-VAUGHN
COMPANY
ELEMENTARY • SECONDARY • ADULT • LIBRARY

About the Authors

MARTHA K. RESNICK is an experienced elementary teacher, formerly a Reading Resource Teacher with the Baltimore City Schools. She has served as a cooperative practice teacher, training student teachers from many colleges. Mrs. Resnick received her master's degree in education at Loyola College.

CAROLYN J. HYATT has taught elementary, secondary, and adult education classes. She was formerly a Senior Teacher with the Baltimore City Schools. Mrs. Hyatt received her master's degree in education at Loyola College.

Reading Comprehension Series

Wags & Tags

Claws & Paws

Gills & Bills

Manes & Reins

Bones & Stones

Swells & Shells

Heights & Flights

Trails & Dales

Acknowledgments

Illustrated by Rosemarie Fox-Hicks, Sue Durban, and Holly Cooper

Cover design Linda Adkins Design

Cover photograph © Comstock

All photographs used with permission. Interior photographs: © 1988 Chicago Zoological Society; © 1988 E. R. Degginger/Hillstrom Stock Photo; © 1988 Graphic Masters Inc./David Roth; © 1988 Kenji Kerins; © 1988 Alan G. Nelson/Root Resources

ISBN 0-8114-1343-8

Contents

Look at this animal.
Its feathers look like
a black and white suit.
It walks on two feet.
It has a bill.
It cannot fly, but it swims.
Its flippers help it swim.
It is a penguin, a bird
that lives on ice.

It was a dark, cold winter day. Many penguins left the water and met on the ice. The penguins made a lot of noise. They called to each other.

Mr. Penguin called to Mrs. Penguin. Mrs. Penguin heard his voice. They met and walked.

After several days, Mrs. Penguin laid one egg on the ice. It was time to make a nest for the baby penguin egg.

Mr. Penguin rolled the egg onto his two feet. His stomach feathers covered the egg and kept it warm.

Soon Mrs. Penguin called "Good-by!" She and the other mother penguins went into the sea. They went to eat fish.

The dads stayed on the ice to care for the eggs. They kept the eggs warm for many weeks. They ate nothing. They got very skinny.

One day, the father penguins were talking.

"Where are the mothers?" one penguin asked. "It's time for the eggs to open."

Another penguin said, "I hope they are safe."

Surprise! The next day, the eggs started to open. The little baby penguins began to make noise. The dads were happy.

But where were the mother penguins?

1. Where did Mr. Penguin keep his egg?

_____ a. in the mud

_____ b. on his feet

_____ c. on his bill

2. When did the mother penguins go away?

_____ a. after the babies came out of the eggs

_____ b. before they laid the eggs

_____ c. after they laid the eggs

3. While the father penguins held their eggs, when did they eat?

_____ a. when it was dark

_____ b. never

_____ c. when they had an egg sitter

4. Where were the mother penguins?

_____ a. getting food from the sea

_____ b. getting skinny

_____ c. at the store getting food

5. What is a good name for this story?

_____ a. A Funny Nest

_____ b. A Nest in a Tree

_____ c. Mother Penguin Sits on the Eggs

6. When did the penguins meet on the ice?

_____ a. in the winter

_____ b. never

_____ c. when it was warm

7. What is something penguins never do?

_____ a. swim _____ b. make noises _____ c. fly

8. What animals eat penguins?

_____ a. horses _____ b. sharks _____ c. cows

B **Draw lines to match these.**
One is done for you.

ice

1. what your ears did

stomach

2. something to put on

feathers

3. something very cold

voice

4. very thin

heard

5. what you hear when
someone talks

each

6. what covers all birds

suit

7. more than two

skinny

8. where food goes
when you eat

several

What happened first? Next? Last?
Put 1, 2, and 3 in the boxes.

[ ] Mr. Penguin kept the egg warm.

[ ] The egg began to open.

[ ] Mrs. Penguin laid an egg.

D **Circle the right word. One is done for you.**

1. The two penguins | men / (met) | there.

2. I heard her | very / voice | .

3. Penguins' feathers look like a | seven / suit | .

4. One egg was laid by | each / reach | bird.

5. The eggs must be | worm / warm | .

6. All birds have feathers and | bills / pills | .

2

Surprise! The baby penguins came out of the eggs. Another surprise! The same day, the mother penguins came back from the sea. They were fat from eating many fish. They came back to care for the baby penguins.

Mrs. Penguin saw all the dads and baby penguins. They were all making noise. But Mrs. Penguin knew Mr. Penguin's voice. She walked right to him.

Mr. Penguin said, "Meet our new little girl, Penny."

"Oh," said Mrs. Penguin. "What a pretty little baby she is!"

Baby Penny was hungry. Hungry penguin babies peck on their parents' bills. Then the parents put food in the babies' mouths. Mrs. Penguin fed Baby Penny.

"I'm very hungry, too," said Mr. Penguin. "Now it's my turn to eat."

"Us, too," said all the father penguins. They waved their skinny flippers and said, "Good-by." They all went in to the water to find food.

For two weeks, Mr. Penguin and all the father penguins ate fish. They ate fish night and day. They ate fish heads, fish tails, fish fins, and fish gills. They got round and fat. Their stomachs were full.

Then the fathers were ready to swim home. They were ready to help care for the baby penguins.

A shark saw fat Mr. Penguin swimming home. The shark followed Mr. Penguin.

Mr. Penguin moved down, down in to the deep water. The shark went swimming after him.

Quick as a flash, Mr. Penguin zoomed up, up. His flippers moved as fast as the wind.

He rolled onto his stomach. He slid through the water right up to the icy shore.

The hungry shark's mouth opened. He reached for Mr. Penguin's tail feathers. The shark was unlucky. Mr. Penguin, quick as a flash, slid out of the water. He zoomed over the ice on his stomach.

He heard Mrs. Penguin's voice. He heard Baby Penny's voice. He slid right over to them.

A **Which one is right? Put a ✔ by it.**

1. How was Mrs. Penguin different when she came back?

_____ a. She was round and fat.

_____ b. She was very skinny.

_____ c. She was hungry.

2. When did Mr. Penguin go to eat?

_____ a. the week before the egg opened

_____ b. when the egg was on his feet

_____ c. after the egg opened

3. Why did Mr. Penguin go away from Mrs. Penguin?

_____ a. He wanted to play.

_____ b. He needed a new suit.

_____ c. He needed food.

4. Why do you think Mr. Penguin slid on his stomach?

_____ a. His feet hurt.

_____ b. It was quicker than walking on ice.

_____ c. It was the only way he could move.

5. What is the best name for this story?

_____ a. Penny Gets Away from a Shark

_____ b. The Baby Penguin Turns Around

_____ c. Mr. and Mrs. Penguin Take Turns

B Read the words in the Word Box. Read the sentences. Write the word that belongs in each sentence.

Word Box	flippers followed	parents another	waved

1. The baby _____ his parents.

2. Penguins swim with their _____.

3. The moms _____ good-by.

4. Your mom and dad are your _____.

10

C **Read the sentences. Put an X next to ones that are not right. Put a ✔ next to the ones that are right.**

_____ 1. Penguins have warm fur.

_____ 2. Mother penguins keep the eggs on their feet.

_____ 3. The parents take turns helping the baby.

_____ 4. Penguins fly quickly.

_____ 5. Penguins feathers are black and white.

_____ 6. The penguin slid on his stomach quick as a flash.

D **Here is a penguin. Draw a line from each word to its picture.**

1. bill   2. head

3. stomach   4. flipper

5. feet   6. tail

E **Circle the right word.**

1. The penguins waved their | flippers / followed | .

2. Mrs. Penguin did not come back the | some / same | day.

3. Penguins swim quick as a | feather / flash | .

4. Fish have | gills / bills | .

11

Sunday afternoon Pedro said, "I will not go! I do not want to go to Nita's party!"

"Why not?" asked his mother.

Pedro told her, "Nita asked **nine** girls and **two** boys to come."

Mother said, "Think how unhappy the other boy will be if you are not there."

"I don't care!" yelled Pedro.

But his mother took him to the door. She gave him the gift for Nita.

"Good-bye, Pedro," Mother said.

Then Pedro went around to the kitchen door. No one saw him go back into the house.

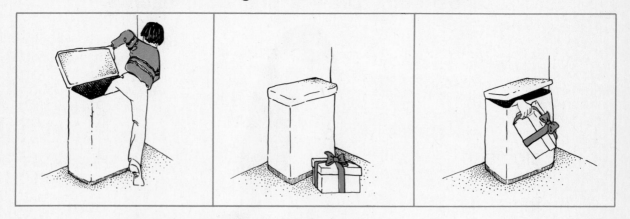

Chico, the dog, walked by.

Mother hugged Chico. Father hugged Chico. They said, "What a good dog."

Pedro said, "I can never hide from Chico!"

1. What did Pedro do first?

    _____ a. He hid.

    _____ b. He said, "I do not want to go."

    _____ c. He went in the back door.

2. Where did Chico go?

    _____ a. to Nita's party

    _____ b. to the doghouse

    _____ c. to a woman and a man

3. Why didn't Pedro want to go?

    _____ a. too many gifts

    _____ b. too many boys

    _____ c. too many girls

4. Why did Pedro get a gift for Nita?

    _____ a. It was Nita's birthday.

    _____ b. Nita was very sick.

    _____ c. Nita was going away.

5. When was the party?

    _____ a. morning

    _____ b. afternoon

    _____ c. night

6. What day was the party?

_____ a. Saturday   _____ b. Sunday   _____ c. Friday

7. How did Chico know where Pedro was?

_____ a. Mother told him.

_____ b. Pedro told him.

_____ c. He smelled Pedro.

8. What is the best name for this story?

_____ a. Pedro Hides

_____ b. Looking for Chico

_____ c. Nita's Gift

B **Draw lines to match these. One is done for you.**

1. go where no one can see you

2. not this one

3. said a question

4. comes after ten

5. not in front

asked

how

hide

eleven

other

back

14

C What happened first? Next? Last? Put **1, 2, 3, 4,** and **5** in the boxes.

D Write **yes** or **no** in the box. One is done for you.

1. Nita is the pet dog.

no

2. Pedro has two feet.

3. Chico can read a book.

4. The gift was for Nita.

5. Nita asked nine girls to the party.

6. Mother took Chico to the party.

7. Chico found Pedro.

Tuesday Sally and Sam were playing outdoors in the snow. They made a little snowman.

The snowman's eyes were buttons. His nose was a carrot. His mouth was two sticks.

"Let's put a cap on his head," said Sally. "He is beautiful!"

"The sun is out," said Sam. "It can melt the snowman."

The children took the little snowman into the kitchen. They stopped up the sink. They put him in the sink. They put ice all around him.

"He will not melt now," laughed Sam.

"Let's go play at Yong Cha's house until Dad comes home," said Sally. Out they ran.

All afternoon Sally and Sam were gone. Drip, drip went the water into the sink. Melt, melt went the snowman in the sink.

When Dad and the children came home, they saw a sink full of water. A carrot and two buttons floated in the water.

What do you think happened? What do you think they had to do?

A **Which one is right? Put a ✔ by it.**

1. What did the children do first?

   _____ a. They went to Yong Cha's house.

   _____ b. They took a snowman into the kitchen.

   _____ c. They put a cap on the snowman.

2. Why was the snowman in the kitchen?

   _____ a. to keep the kitchen cold

   _____ b. to keep the snowman from melting

   _____ c. to keep the snowman warm

3. What was a nose for the snowman?

   _____ a. a button

   _____ b. a carrot

   _____ c. a stick

4. Where did the children go?

   _____ a. to get Dad

   _____ b. to school

   _____ c. to play with a friend

5. What was floating in the sink?

   _____ a. a carrot and two buttons

   _____ b. a button and a boot

   _____ c. a carrot and a boot

6. Which picture do you think fits the end of the story?

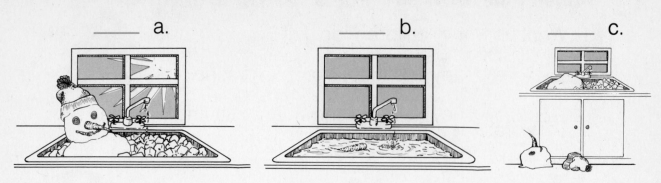

_____ a.   _____ b.   _____ c.

7. What do you think Sally and Sam had to do next?

_____ a. go swimming

_____ b. take a bath

_____ c. clean the sink

8. What is the story about?

_____ a. making a snowman with Dad

_____ b. a talking snowman

_____ c. the sun melting a snowman

B. Draw lines to match these.

1. good to look at

2. becomes water

3. an orange food

4. a part of you

5. stay on top of the water

6. not in the house

7. It holds water in the kitchen.

sink

beautiful

outdoors

float

melts

drip

carrot

nose

C Circle the right word. One is done for you.

1. Dad said, " ~~I'm~~ (I'll) go with you."

2. Sally said, " That's / I'm my snowman."

3. Sam said, " It's / Let's go to Yong Cha's house."

4. Dad said, "Come home with my / me ."

5. They said, " I / We must stop the water."

D Read about where each child lives. Then write the first letter of the child's name on the right house.

Sam and Sally live on Blue Street. Their friends live on Blue Street, too.

1. Carlos said, "My house has a fence around it."

2. Kim said, "You can swim in back of my house."

3. Sam said, "We have a doghouse out back."

4. Yong Cha said, "I live next door to Sam."

5

Last Saturday there was a boat race. Eight boats were in it. The boats had to race across the lake. Boats that got to the other side first were winners.

The boats were in a line. They started off in a hurry. A big red boat went fast. A yellow boat went faster. The other boats were in back of them.

Then a fire started on the red boat. People stopped the red boat to put out the fire.

The white boat went too near the land. It got in the mud. It did not get across the lake.

The yellow boat bumped into the brown boat. They were out of the race.

A pink boat got to the other side first. The green boat came in second. Next came a purple boat. It was third. An old orange boat was the last in the race.

All the boats that got across the lake were winners. People on those boats won some money.

A **Which one is right? Put a ✔ by it.**

1. What is this story about?

_____ a. children in a race

_____ b. a boat race

_____ c. a car race

2. Where was this race?

_____ a. on a playground

_____ b. on a street

_____ c. in the water

3. How many boats had to stop?

_____ a. four _____ b. three _____ c. eight

4. What happened to the white boat?

_____ a. It had a fire.

_____ b. It came in first.

_____ c. It got in the mud.

5. What happened to the brown boat?

_____ a. It went too near the land.

_____ b. It was hit by the yellow boat.

_____ c. It had a fire.

6. What did the winners get?

_____ a. cups _____ b. money _____ c. boats

B How did they come in? Color the boats.
Write the names of the colors.

1. first   2. second   3. third   4. last

_____   _____   _____   _____

- - - - -   - - - - -   - - - - -   - - - - -

_____   _____   _____   _____

C Draw lines to match these.

1. some water   bumped

2. ran into something   third

3. something very hot   across

4. a color   lake

5. after the first two   Saturday

6. the one that comes in first   orange

7. from one side to the other   fire

8. a row of things   winner

                                                          line

D **Put an X on the word that does not belong. One is done for you.**

1. Wednesday   Monday   sp~~r~~ing   Saturday

2. runner   winner   player   butter

3. lake   pond   boat   water

4. third   tiger   dog   worm

5. ten   three   tree   nine

6. grass   tree   second   flower

7. boat   fire   car   bus

E **Fun Time! Can you do this?**

1. Color the second boat pink.

2. Put a ✔ on the next to the last one.

3. Color the first boat purple.

4. Put an **X** under the last boat.

5. Color the third boat orange.

6. Put a box around the second boat.

7. Color the tall boats in the middle green.

8. How many boats did you color green? _____

A **Read this story. Check the right answers.**

One warm day, Carlos and Pedro were at the zoo. A zoo helper was showing the people a father penguin. The dad had no egg to take care of. The zoo helper put a hot dog roll next to the father penguin. The father penguin put it on his feet. His feathers kept it warm.

The zoo helper said, "The penguin wants a baby to come out of the roll."

Pedro, Carlos, and all the people laughed.

1. What do you think happened next?

_____ a. A baby penguin came out of the roll.

_____ b. The penguin made a nest for the roll.

_____ c. A baby seal came out of the roll.

2. What do you know about Carlos and Pedro?

_____ a. They lived in a zoo.

_____ b. They ate hot dogs at the zoo.

_____ c. They had fun at the zoo.

3. When did this story happen?

_____ a. one cold night

_____ b. one warm night

_____ c. one warm day

B Here is a snowman. Draw a line from each word to its picture.

1. buttons

3. carrot

5. sticks

7. cap

2. head

4. eyes

6. nose

8. mouth

C Write the names of the children next to the pictures.

1. _____

2. _____

3. _____

4. _____

5. _____

6. _____

1. Jill is next to the last.

2. Sam is right after the third.

3. Pedro is the first.

4. Sally is the second.

5. Dan is the last.

6. Andy is not here.

7. Ann is the third.

D **Can you guess the riddles? Circle the right words.**

1. It is wet. It can be hot or cold.
   You can drink it. It is in food.
   You can give it to flowers.
   What is it?

   milk   water   dog

2. It is on you. It helps you eat. It
   helps you talk. What is it?

   milk   melt   mouth

3. I have four feet and a tail.
   Sometimes I take care of the house.
   I can be black or white or brown.
   I wag my tail and say, "Bow-wow."
   I like to play with a ball.
   What am I?

   a dog   a bird   an ant

4. Sometimes I have it. Sometimes you
   have it. I can give it to someone.
   Someone can give it to you. No one
   likes to get it. It makes you sick.
   What is it?

   a hot dog   a cold   a hot

E Read the words in the Word Box.
Write the words next to the meanings.

Word Box

wins	fur	stomach	sink
third	across	feathers	slid
melts	gills	last	

1. comes after second

_____

2. from side to side

_____

3. a part of your body

_____

4. a part of a fish

_____

5. something in the kitchen

_____

6. becomes water

_____

7. comes in first

_____

8. what covers a bird

_____

9. what covers cats

_____

10. at the end of the line

_____

6

On Thursday evening, Janet took her little brother, Jay, to the big ball park. Jay was eight years old. Jay didn't understand the ball game. But he liked to sit outdoors and yell. He liked to eat hot dogs and popcorn.

Jay had a hot dog in one hand. He had a box of popcorn in his lap. He had a hot dog next to him, too. Jay was very happy.

The batter hit the ball. The ball came flying over to the people.

"It's a home run!" yelled all the people.

"I want to get that ball!" yelled Janet.

People got ready to grab the ball. Everyone wanted to catch the ball. But not Jay! He was eating. He did not want to catch the ball.

Down came the ball! Did it fly into the hands waiting for it? No! It came down on Jay's lap on top of his popcorn! The hot dog and popcorn fell to the ground. But Jay had the ball!

"The boy who didn't want the ball got it!" said Janet.

All Jay said was, "Let's get more popcorn!"

A **Which one is right? Put a ✔ by it.**

1. When did they go to the ball game?

____ a. morning ____ b. noon ____ c. night

2. How old was Jay?

____ a. seven ____ b. nine ____ c. eight

3. Why did Jay go to the ball game?

____ a. to eat hot dogs and popcorn

____ b. to get a ball

____ c. to play ball

4. Where did the ball go?

____ a. out of the ball park

____ b. into Janet's hands

____ c. into Jay's lap

5. What do you think happened next?

____ a. Jay started to cry.

____ b. Jay let Janet have the ball.

____ c. Jay hit a home run.

6. What is the best name for this story?

____ a. The Ball Hits Janet

____ b. A Surprise Hot Dog

____ c. A Surprise Ball

B **Draw lines to match these.**

1. to know all about

2. a white food

3. what your legs make when you sit down

4. one who hits the ball with a bat

5. a ball hit very far

6. a boy in your family

7. not in the house

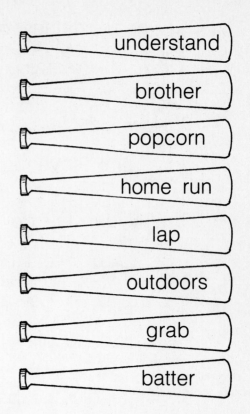

understand

brother

popcorn

home run

lap

outdoors

grab

batter

C **Who is talking? Write the name. One is done for you.**

Jay

1. "That is not a home run," said Jay to Janet.

2. "Jay, we will go this evening," said Janet.

3. Jay said, "I don't understand this game, Janet."

4. "Catch that ball!" yelled Janet. "Jay, help catch it!"

5. "No, Janet," said Jay, "that is not my hot dog."

30

D Find the sentence that goes with each picture. Write the letter on the line.

1. _____ 2. _____ 3. _____

4. _____ 5. _____ 6. _____

7. _____ 8. _____ 9. _____

a. This game does not use a ball.
b. The food is on her lap.
c. The batter is ready to hit the ball.
d. The book is on his lap.
e. Everyone wants to catch the ball.
f. The people are getting ready to swim.
g. The popcorn and hot dog fell to the ground.
h. Someone is catching the ball.
i. The people are getting ready to fly.
j. The popcorn fell to the ground.

7

One spring day, Ann and Andy were planting seeds. Their little brother, Billy, did not want to help.

A woman came by. She looked at Billy and said, "Here are five seeds. If you plant the five seeds, you will get a big surprise."

Billy wanted to know what the surprise was. He planted the seeds in back of the dog house.

Soon three little plants came up. Little leaves were on them. Billy watered them every day. The plants got bigger. They got big leaves on them. Then they began to go all over the ground like this.

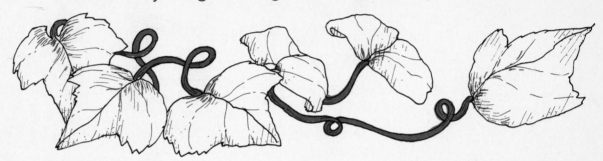

Then pretty yellow flowers came out on the plants. Under the flowers were little green balls. Every day the green balls got bigger. Then the green balls became yellow.

Soon the yellow balls were very, very big. Now they became orange. They looked like this.

Billy and the children laughed. They saw what the big surprise was.

Do you know what Billy had planted?

A **Which one is right? Put a ✔ by it.**

1. What were the surprise plants?

    _____ a. water plants

    _____ b. pumpkins

    _____ c. new flowers

2. How many of Billy's seeds did not grow?

    _____ a. five _____ b. three _____ c. two

3. Why did Billy plant the seeds?

    _____ a. He liked to see flowers come up.

    _____ b. He wanted to know what the surprise was.

    _____ c. He wanted to help his family.

4. Where did Billy get the seeds?

    _____ a. at the store

    _____ b. from his mother

    _____ c. from a woman

5. What came out of the plants first?

    _____ a. leaves

    _____ b. flowers

    _____ c. yellow balls

6. What color were the flowers?

    _____ a. white _____ b. yellow _____ c. pink

7. Where did Billy plant the seeds?

_____ a. in a window box

_____ b. under a tree

_____ c. in back of the dog house

8. What is the best name for this story?

_____ a. The Pretty Yellow Flowers

_____ b. The Pretty Woman

_____ c. The Surprise Plants

B **Draw lines to match these.**

1. said, "Ha, ha, ha!"

2. an orange food

3. a girl who grew up

4. nice to look at

5. thing a plant grows from

6. grew into

7. land we walk on

8. putting it into the ground
   to grow

woman

brother

laughed

pumpkin

planting

pretty

ground

seed

became

C **Find the sentence that means the same as the first one. Put a ✔ by it.**

1. Billy, Ann, and Andy were planting seeds.

_____ a. They were putting seeds in the ground.

_____ b. She was putting seeds in the ground.

2. Five little seeds were in the woman's hand.

_____ a. The woman had a seed in her hand.

_____ b. The woman had some seeds in her hand.

3. Billy watered the plants every day.

_____ a. Billy put water on the plants two times.

_____ b. Billy put water on the plants day after day.

4. The seeds were planted in the spring.

_____ a. The seeds were planted in the summer.

_____ b. The seeds were planted before summer.

5. The yellow flowers fell off. Under them were little green balls.

_____ a. Little green balls were under the flowers.

_____ b. The green balls became yellow flowers.

6. The children found out what the surprise was.

_____ a. The children knew that the surprise seeds were pumpkin seeds.

_____ b. The children did not know what the seeds were.

8

On Thursday snow fell. Marcy and Dan went outdoors. The trees and grass were white with snow. The children's boots made marks in the snow. Dan looked back to see them.

"Our boots make funny tracks in the snow," said Dan.

"Look over there," said Marcy. "An animal has walked here before us."

They saw tracks in the snow.

"Let's see where the animal went," said Dan.

"Maybe we can find out what animal makes tracks like these," said Marcy.

The children followed the tracks into the woods. The tracks went over to an old tree that had fallen to the ground.

"Look under that tree!" said Dan. "It's a pretty little black and white cat."

"Let's take the cat home. It must be very cold," said Marcy.

The children ran to the old tree. But they stopped before they got up to it.

"Oh! Oh!" they yelled. "That's no cat! Let's get away from here."

Dan said, "If we get too near to it, we may smell a very bad smell."

What animal had made the tracks in the snow?

A Which one is right? Put a ✔ by it.

1. What animal did they see?

_____ a. cat   _____ b. squirrel   _____ c. skunk

2. How did they know an animal was near by?

_____ a. They saw its tracks.

_____ b. They could hear it walking.

_____ c. The animal said, "Mew, mew."

3. Where did they see the animal?

_____ a. in the leaves

_____ b. under an old tree

_____ c. under a fence

4. When did the snow fall?

_____ a. Monday   _____ b. Thursday   _____ c. Friday

5. What can this animal do if you get too near?

_____ a. It can bark at you.

_____ b. It can bite you.

_____ c. It can let out a bad smell.

6. What is the best name for this story?

_____ a. An Animal's Spots

_____ b. The Tracks of the Skunk

_____ c. The Tracks of the Fox

B Draw lines to match these.

1. the day before Friday

2. marks that feet make

3. down on the ground

4. went in back of

5. place with many trees

6. animal with four feet

7. making us laugh

fallen

followed

funny

smell

skunk

Thursday

tracks

woods

C What do you know about skunks?
Circle the right ones.

1. Which is the skunk?

2. How many feet do skunks have?   two   four

3. Do skunks talk?   yes   no

4. Do skunks read?   yes   no

5. Do skunks have green spots?   yes   no

6. Can we ride on a skunk?   yes   no

7. Are skunks white and black?   yes   no

8. Do skunks put on boots?   yes   no

D **Circle the right word for each story.**

1. The skunk did not want people to catch her.
   She went under the fallen tree.
   She ____ there.

   had   hid   did

---

2. The big bear ran to the old tree. A skunk lived
   in the old tree. The bear surprised her. Then
   the skunk surprised the bear! She let out a
   bad ____.

   sell   spell   smell

---

3. There was an old tree by Dan's window. Every
   morning Dan looked at it. One day the tree
   was not there. It was on the ground. The tree
   had ____ down.

   fallen   rested   smelled

---

4. White snow was all over the ground. Dan put on
   his hat and coat. He went out to play. He could
   not walk in the snow. Dan said, "I forgot
   my ____."

   books   boots   bugs

---

5. Marcy walked in the snow. Her boots made marks
   where she walked. Dan wanted to find Marcy.
   Dan found her by looking at Marcy's ____.

   trees   backs   tracks

9

Why don't people like us? We are pretty animals. We help people.

We help by eating bugs that hurt people. We eat rats and mice, too. We hunt for food at night. We eat things that people do not want.

We never try to get into houses as mice do. We never run after people as tigers do. We do not climb trees as squirrels do.

We skunks like to be with other skunks. We do not try to live with people. We stay away from other animals. We live in old trees or under the ground.

We smell good if you do not put your hands on us. Be careful near us, and you will not smell us. We let out our bad smell if someone wants to hurt us.

We want you to be careful and not run after us. Stay away from us, and we will stay away from you. But we like to help you. Please like us!

A **Which one is right? Put a ✔ by it.**

1. When do skunks come out to eat?

_____ a. morning _____ b. noon _____ c. night

2. What would a skunk eat?

_____ a. a fly _____ b. a bag _____ c. a house

3. How do skunks help people?

_____ a. by looking pretty

_____ b. by eating mice

_____ c. by smelling nice

4. When will a skunk smell bad?

_____ a. when you try to catch it

_____ b. all the time

_____ c. never

5. What do skunks want people to do for them?

_____ a. play with them

_____ b. keep away from them

_____ c. bring them into the house

6. What is the best name for this story?

_____ a. A Bad Animal

_____ b. A Careful Animal

_____ c. Helpers to People

B Draw lines to match the opposites.
One is done for you.

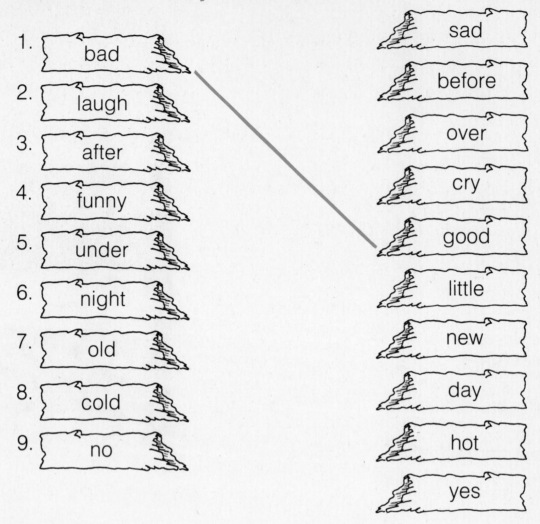

1. bad
2. laugh
3. after
4. funny
5. under
6. night
7. old
8. cold
9. no

sad
before
over
cry
good
little
new
day
hot
yes

C Can you guess the riddles? Circle the right word.

1. This is an animal.
It has four feet.
It is a friend to us.
You may have one
as a pet.
It eats mice.
It says, "Mew, mew."
What is it?

cow   skunk   cat

2. This is a place.
Many trees are here.
Many animals live here.
Skunks and birds are
here.
Bugs, worms, and ants
live here, too.
What is this place?

store   woods   school

42

3. This is someone who likes you.
It is someone that you like, too.
This someone helps you.
It is someone you want to help.
This someone will not hurt you.
Who is it?

       friend   fire   four

4. This is on you. It smells things.
It can smell food cooking.
It can smell pretty flowers.
It can get red and cold in winter.
What is it?

       mouth   ear   nose

D **Which is the right word? Circle it.**

1. Some animals can ____ fast.

    swim   swimming

2. Skunks help us by ____ bugs that hurt us.

    eat   eating

3. A skunk likes to ____ with other skunks.

    stay   staying

4. The skunk let out a bad ____ at the fox.

    smell   smelling

5. Skunks ____ for food at night.

    hunt   hunting

6. Some people ____ skunks are pretty.

    think   thinking

10

Tom, Bob, and Jack were going fishing on Friday afternoon. They went out that morning to dig up some worms. The boys put the worms into a can. They left the can on the kitchen table. Jack's grandmother saw the worms.

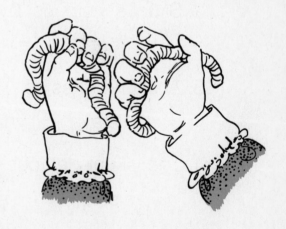

"Oh, no!" yelled Grandmother. "Get those things out of here!"

Jack said, "Don't you like worms, Grandmother?"

"No!" said Grandmother. The boys laughed.

After lunch, the three boys left to go fishing. They saw Betty and Jill.

"Let's see if the girls will yell," said Bob.

"Let's put worms on them," said Tom. "It will be so funny."

Jack said to the girls, "Close your eyes. Hold out your hands. I have something for you."

Jill and Betty put out their hands. Jack pulled four worms out of the can. He put two worms in each girl's hands.

Then the boys got a surprise. Betty and Jill did not run or yell! They held the worms.

"Don't you want us to take away the worms?" asked Jack. "Grandmother didn't like them."

"No, we like worms," said the girls.

Betty and Jill took the four worms and went fishing.

1. When did this happen?

_____ a. Sunday _____ b. Friday _____ c. Tuesday

2. When did the boys dig up the worms?

_____ a. morning _____ b. afternoon _____ c. night

3. What is the story about?

_____ a. The boys got a lot of fish.

_____ b. Grandmother surprised the girls.

_____ c. The girls surprised the boys.

4. Where did Grandmother see the worms?

_____ a. in the yard

_____ b. in the girls' hands

_____ c. on the table

5. Why did Grandmother yell?

_____ a. The worms got away.

_____ b. She did not like worms.

_____ c. The boys were eating worms.

6. When did the boys eat lunch?

_____ a. before they got worms

_____ b. after they went fishing

_____ c. after they got worms

7. What did the girls do with the worms?

_____ a. yelled at them

_____ b. put them back in the can

_____ c. went fishing

8. What does this story show us?

_____ a. Everyone likes worms.

_____ b. No one likes worms.

_____ c. Some people like worms.

9. What is the best name for this story?

_____ a. How Worms Help Us

_____ b. How To Fish

_____ c. Who Likes Worms?

B **Draw lines to match these.**

fishing

1. a little animal

Friday

2. your mother's mother

grandmother

3. comes after Thursday

left

4. keep something in your hand

worm

5. to shut

close

6. went away

hold

C **What is going on in the picture? Put an X by the sentence that goes with the picture.**

1. _____ a. Four cans are on the table.

   _____ b. Three cans are in the yard.

   _____ c. Two cans are on the table.

2. _____ a. A girl is pulling a worm.

   _____ b. A grandmother is pulling flowers.

   _____ c. A bird is pulling a worm.

3. _____ a. The boys held some fish.

   _____ b. The boys held some worms.

   _____ c. The fish held some boys.

4. _____ a. Flowers are in the back yard.

   _____ b. Fish are in the back yard.

   _____ c. Grandmother is in the back yard.

5. _____ a. Fish are swimming in the water.

   _____ b. Fish are yelling in the water.

   _____ c. Worms are swimming in the water.

A **Why are these words together? Pick a name for these words from the box. Write the names on the right lines.**

numbers	foods	people
places	colors	animals

1. _____

brother   woman
batter   children
grandmother

2. _____

popcorn   fish
oranges   pumpkin
hot dog

3. _____

ball park   woods
kitchen   school

4. _____

black   white
orange   yellow

B **Draw lines to match these.**

1. boy in your family

2. said, "Ha, ha!"

3. not in the house

4. girl who grew up

5. day before Friday

6. to shut

outdoors
orange
close
brother
woman
laughed
Thursday

C **What do you know about skunks and worms? Circle the right ones.**

1. Which one will let out a bad smell?

2. Do skunks have two tails?   yes   no

3. Does a skunk fly at night?   yes   no

4. Are skunks land animals?   yes   no

5. Can skunks help people?   yes   no

6. Can a worm eat a fish?   yes   no

7. Do worms run very fast?   yes   no

8. Do worms hide in the grass?   yes   no

9. Can we ride on a worm?   yes   no

D **Can you guess the riddles? Circle the right word.**

1. This is very hot.
   It looks yellow.
   It helps plants grow.
   We see it in the day.
   What is it?

   sun moon snow

2. It is cold and white.
   Put it in a cup.
   It is good to drink.
   We get it from cows.
   What is it?

   snow rain milk

3. This animal is careful.
   It never runs too fast.
   It pulls its legs and
   head into its shell.
   What is it?

   skunk turtle squirrel

4. This animal likes trees.
   It climbs to tree tops.
   It eats nuts.
   It lives in the park.
   What is it?

   turtle squirrel skunk

49

E **Circle the one word that fits both sentences.**

cold   hold   sold

1. Get a good ____ on the rope.

2. Can you ____ any more food?

plant   place   play

3. Put some water on the lettuce ____.

4. Let's ____ some pumpkin seeds.

far   fell   fall

5. This ____ we will rake the leaves.

6. Did you ____ down on the playground?

F **Who is talking? Write the name.**

_____ 1. "Don't you like worms, Grandmother?" asked Jack.

_____ 2. Betty said to Jill, "I see Tom, Bob, and Jack over there."

_____ 3. Bob said, "Let's see if Betty and Jill will yell."

_____ 4. "Do you want us to take away the worms, Betty?" asked Tom.

_____ 5. "No," said Jill, "Betty and I like worms."

G **What is funny about the pictures? Put a ✔ by the funny sentences.**

1.

_____ a. The mice are going across the lake on a pumpkin.

_____ b. The mice are going across the lake on a boat.

2.

_____ a. The skunk left its tracks in the snow.

_____ b. The skunk's tracks look like hands.

3.

_____ a. The worm is eating the fish.

_____ b. The fish is eating the worm.

4.

_____ a. Father Robin gives the bird a worm.

_____ b. Father Robin gives the tiger a worm.

5.

_____ a. Jay has a bat in his hot dog bun.

_____ b. Jay has a hot dog to eat.

11

Karen, Mai, and Ann went to the mall on Saturday morning. They wanted to get some T-shirts. Karen's big brother Ray took the girls in his new car. They got there at eleven o'clock.

"I'll be back to pick you up at two o'clock," said Ray. "Meet me here at the Water Street door."

The three friends walked around the mall. They looked in some stores. They had some pizza at the food stand. Then they went to the T-shirt store.

> Get your T-shirts here!
> We have them all ~
> Large and Small!
> Your name added free!

Karen liked to swim. She saw a T-shirt with a picture of a large penguin. "That's for me!" she said.

Mai's shirt had a picture of a tiny fox. Ann got one with a shark.

It was almost two o'clock. The girls ran fast to the Water Street door. They were just in time. Ray was just getting there.

A Which one is right? Put a ✔ by it.

1. Why did the girls go to the mall?

_____ a. They went to help Karen's brother.

_____ b. They wanted to get new T-shirts.

_____ c. It was a rainy day.

2. What time do you think the girls went to the mall?

_____ a. at night

_____ b. on Sunday

_____ c. in the morning

3. What is the best title for this story?

_____ a. Fun at the Mall

_____ b. Ray's New Shoes

_____ c. A Rainy Walk Home

4. What happened first in the story?

_____ a. The girls got their names on T-shirts.

_____ b. The girls ate.

_____ c. The girls ran to the Water Street door.

5. When did the girls have to meet Ray?

_____ a. at five o'clock

_____ b. at two o'clock

_____ c. at eleven o'clock

6. What meal did the girls eat at the mall?

_____ a. ice cream _____ b. lunch _____ c. dinner

7. How did the girls go into the mall?

_____ a. at the big blue door

_____ b. at the door on Beach Street

_____ c. at the door on Water Street

B Write each girl's name on her T-shirt. Detective Sharp-Eye says, "Look back in the story. Find the clues. Which T-shirt do you think belongs to Ann? Which to Karen? Which to Mai?"

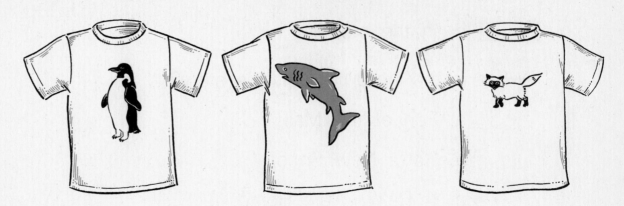

C Draw lines to match these.

1. a place with many stores

2. something to eat

3. the opposite of small

4. something you draw

5. very, very small

6. one more than ten

7. comes before the afternoon

8. a place to go in and out

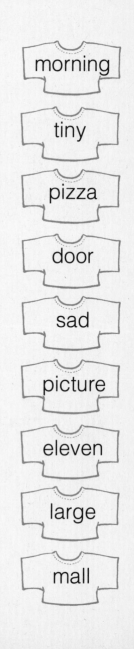

morning

tiny

pizza

door

sad

picture

eleven

large

mall

D **What is funny about the pictures?**
Put a ✔ by the right sentences.

_____ a. There is something heavy on the kangaroo's tail.

_____ b. The kangaroo has a large tail.

_____ a. The desk is too old.

_____ b. The desk is too heavy.

_____ a. The train took people to places far away.

_____ b. The train went swimming.

_____ a. The T-shirt is too large for him.

_____ b. The T-shirt is too small for him.

_____ a. The baby giraffe comes out of a penguin egg.

_____ b. The baby penguin comes out of the egg.

55

On Tuesday evening, the family got home at eight o'clock. There was something on the door.

I was here, but you were out. I hid a surprise gift for you. Look for it.
Love,
Aunt May

The family looked everywhere. Randy hunted in the kitchen. Peggy and Mom ran to the bedroom. Dad hunted in the living room. They all went into the hall. They found nothing!

Then everyone heard something. It came from the bathtub. When the family ran in, they saw

Look in back of this.

This was their surprise gift!

Which one is right? Put a ✔ by it.

1. What were Randy and Peggy looking for?

_____ a. Aunt May   _____ b. a surprise

2. Which sentence is right?

_____ a. Aunt May did not leave a surprise.

_____ b. Aunt May did not get in the house.

_____ c. Aunt May got into the house.

3. Where did the family forget to look?

_____ a. in the living room

_____ b. in the tub

_____ c. on the kitchen sink

4. What happened first?

_____ a. Aunt May got to the house.

_____ b. The family came home.

_____ c. They found an animal.

5. Who looked in the living room?

_____ a. Dad   _____ b. May   _____ c. Peggy

6. What is the best name for this story?

_____ a. A Ball in the Kitchen

_____ b. A New Living Room

_____ c. A Bird in the Bathtub

B Draw lines to match these.

aunt

1. a place for a bath   tub

2. put where no one could see   hall

3. something the ears did   heard

4. part of a house   yard

5. Mom's sister   hid

6. something around the house   gift

C Here is the Table of Contents page of a book. Use it to answer the questions.

1. On which page will you

   find *Mr. Robin*? _____

2. On which page is the
   last story in the book? _____

3. How many stories are in

   this book? _____

Stories

4. On which page does

   A Surprise start? _____

5. Which story starts on page 2?

   _____

   -

D **Peggy and Randy looked for something. They went all around the house. Look at this map to see how they went. Follow the numbers. Circle the words below that tell where they went.**

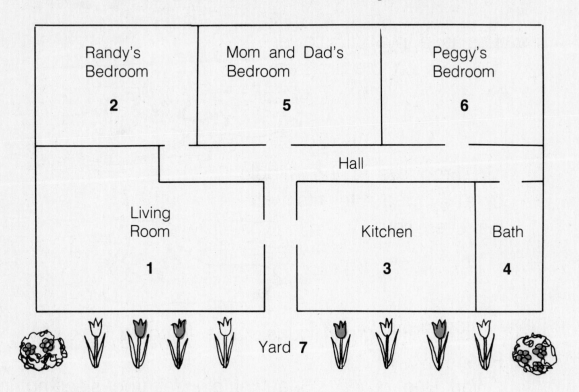

1. Where did they go first?

    living room   kitchen   bath

2. Where did they go last?

    hall   yard   Peggy's bedroom

3. When did they go to Randy's bedroom?

    first   second   third

4. After the kitchen, where did they go next?

    yard   Mom's bedroom   bath

5. After Mom and Dad's bedroom, where did they look next?

    kitchen   yard   Peggy's bedroom

This is a lily pad.
It grows in a pond.

This is a pink lily flower.
It grows on the lily pad.

Mr. Frog sits in the middle
of a lily pad. He sits with
his eyes shut.

Some little green bugs came flying to Pink Lily Pond.

Van Bug called, "See that old, fat frog sleeping in the middle of the pond."

"Let's zoom down and tickle him," said Belle Bug. "Old, fat frogs are not quick."

So all the little green bugs zoomed down to tickle Mr. Frog. They were careful to tickle his back. What fun they had! They laughed until their wings shook! Tickle! Tickle! Tickle!

Some bugs forgot and went too near Mr. Frog's mouth. Surprise! Out came a long tongue! Zap! Zap! The bugs were stuck on that sticky tongue.

Surprise! The sticky tongue rolled back into Mr. Frog's mouth! Mr. Frog's eyes were open now! He had fooled the bugs. He was happy! What a good lunch he was having!

Van Bug said, "So, Belle, never think an old, fat frog cannot be fast! It may fool you!"

A **Which one is right? Put a ✔ by it.**

1. Where did Mr. Frog sit?

_____ a. on a lily pad

_____ b. on a rock

_____ c. in the water

2. Where were the pink lily flowers growing?

_____ a. in water

_____ b. on land

_____ c. in trees

3. What were the bugs careful to do at first?

_____ a. keep the frog's eyes shut

_____ b. stay near the frog's mouth

_____ c. stay in back of the frog

4. Why didn't the bugs fly off the tongue?

_____ a. They wanted to tickle it.

_____ b. They were stuck.

_____ c. The bugs' wings shook.

5. Why did Mr. Frog shut his eyes?

_____ a. to fool the bugs

_____ b. to keep the sun out

_____ c. to sleep

6. What word means **not open**?

_____ a. shut _____ b. quick _____ c. pad

7. What did Van Bug tell Belle?

_____ a. Just eat lily pads.

_____ b. Frogs are not good to eat.

_____ c. Be careful near **all** frogs.

8. What is the best name for this story?

_____ a. The Bugs Fool Mr. Frog

_____ b. The Pretty Pink Lily Pad

_____ c. Mr. Frog's Trick

B **Draw lines to match these.**

1. play a trick on

2. part of a lily plant

3. fast

4. could not get out

5. put your teeth into

6. part of a mouth

7. makes you feel funny

pad

quick

open

tongue

bite

fool

stuck

tickle

C **A dictionary tells you what a word means. Words in a dictionary are put in ABC order.**

eyes The eyes help us see.

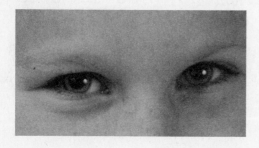

hands The hands help us pick up things.

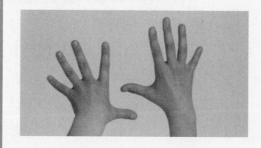

feet We walk and run on our feet.

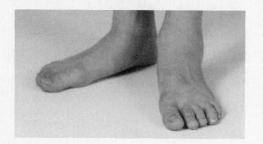

mouth My teeth are in my mouth.

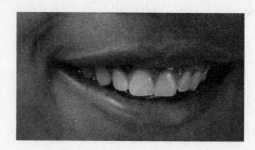

Write the words from the picture dictionary above.

1. What helps us hold this book? _____

2. What helps us look at TV? _____

3. If the word **nose** were on this page, where would it go? Put a ✔ by the right answer.

_____ a. after **mouth**

_____ b. before **mouth**

_____ c. before **eyes**

14

Nicky said, "I'm going to Sam's birthday party next Sunday."

"How old will Sam be?" asked Nicky's big sister, Donna.

"Seven," said Nicky. "His dad made him a cake with seven candles on it."

Nicky told Donna more about the party. "Sam's a big boy now! So his mother let him buy things for the party. Sam asked seven friends to the party. He went out to buy seven funny hats, seven balloons, and seven games for his friends."

"Oh, oh," said Donna. "I think someone will not be happy at Sam's party. He did not buy enough hats, balloons, and games for his friends."

"Yes, he did!" said Nicky.

Then he counted. "Sam asked Ann, Carmen, and Dolly. He asked Tim, Carlos, José, and me. That makes seven of us."

Donna said nothing.

Sunday evening Nicky came home. He yelled, "You were right, Donna. Sam did not have enough hats, balloons, and games. How did you know what would happen?"

His sister said, "If you think, you can work it out, too."

Think like Donna. What did Sam forget? How many balloons, games, and hats did he need?

Which one is right? Put a ✔ by it.

1. How many girls did Sam ask to the party?

   _____ a. four _____ b. three _____ c. no girls

2. How many funny hats did Sam need?

   _____ a. eight _____ b. seven _____ c. nine

3. When did Donna know Sam forgot something?

   _____ a. before the party

   _____ b. after the party

   _____ c. before Sam got the hats

4. What did Sam forget?

   _____ a. to count the people he asked

   _____ b. to count himself

   _____ c. to count the girls

5. What do you think happened at Sam's party?

   _____ a. Every child got a funny hat.

   _____ b. There were too many funny hats.

   _____ c. One child did not get a funny hat.

6. What is the best name for this story?

   _____ a. A Good Party

   _____ b. Sam Forgets Something

   _____ c. Donna Forgets Something

B Draw lines to match these.

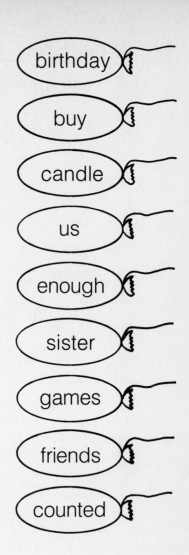

birthday

buy

candle

us

enough

sister

games

friends

counted

1. girl in the family

2. day you were born

3. as many as you need

4. to get things with money

5. people you like

6. something that gives light

7. you and me

8. said, "One, two, three, . . ."

C Draw lines to put the first part of the sentence with the last part.

1. Every year people

2. Birthdays come

3. We have fun with

4. Candles are put

5. People count to find out

6. We eat cake

7. Evening comes

a. one time a year.

b. how many there are.

c. on top of cakes.

d. get older.

e. before night.

f. games and balloons.

g. on a funny hat.

h. after dinner.

D **Circle the best way to end each story.**

1. It is Carmen's birthday. She is four now. She will
be five years old on _____.

   her next birthday   in two years
   her last birthday   last week

2. Sam did not eat all of the cake. He ate
the top of it. He ate the middle. He did not
eat the _____.

   middle   bottom   count

3. Nicky counted the books. There were eight
books. Then he counted the children. He counted
nine children.
Nicky did not have _____.

   every   each   enough

4. Donna got a new plant for her birthday. It was
in a red flower pot. The pot had a hole in the
bottom. Donna put too much water into the pot.
Some of the water came out of the _____.

   flower   hole   birthday

5. One night the lights went out. José and
Carmen could not see in the house. Mother
found something that makes light. Mother
found some _____.

   counts   enough   candles

15

Baby Tiger walked next to his mother all the time. He was afraid of other animals. He began to cry.

Mother Tiger said, "Do not be afraid of other animals, Baby Tiger. Other animals are afraid of us."

Other animals walked by. They looked at the two tigers. They stayed far away from the tigers.

One evening, Mother Tiger was sleeping. Baby Tiger went for a walk alone. He smelled something by a big rock. Baby Tiger looked in back of the rock. He saw an animal that he had never seen before.

The animal looked at Baby Tiger. It went "S—s—s—s—s!" at him.

Baby Tiger said, "You are a funny animal. You have no feet. You have no ears. You are very, very long!"

The funny animal had no feet, but it could move fast. It was quick. Zip! It was all around Baby Tiger. Baby Tiger began to cry.

Mother Tiger came running to help Baby Tiger. Zip! The funny animal went away fast.

Mother Tiger said, "Do not go near that animal again. It can't eat you, but it can bite you!"

A Which one is right? Put a ✔ by it.

1. What happened first?

_____ a. Baby Tiger looked in back of a rock.

_____ b. Baby Tiger talked to the other animal.

_____ c. Baby Tiger smelled something.

2. What animal do you think Baby Tiger saw?

_____ a. bee _____ b. snake _____ c. worm

3. Why do other animals stay away from tigers?

_____ a. Tigers do not smell good.

_____ b. Tigers are afraid of other animals.

_____ c. Tigers can eat other animals.

4. When did this story happen?

_____ a. morning _____ b. noon _____ c. evening

5. What can the funny animal do to tigers?

_____ a. bite them

_____ b. eat them

_____ c. play with them

6. What did we learn from this story?

_____ a. Baby tigers can learn to sleep.

_____ b. Baby animals learn from their mothers.

_____ c. Baby animals are never afraid.

7. What is the best name for this story?

_____ a. Baby Tiger Learns Something New

_____ b. Baby Tiger and the Bees

_____ c. Tigers Are Never Afraid

B **Put a word from the box into each sentence.**

began	snake	bite	other
afraid	quick	smell	around

1. The _____ hid under a rock.

2. Snakes eat _____ animals.

3. Many animals are _____ of tigers.

4. A snake can _____ a tiger.

5. A skunk may let out a bad _____.

C **Read this story. Tell when each one walked by. Put 1, 2, 3, and 4 under the pictures.**

First, a skunk walked by the tigers. Next, a fox ran by them. Then a frog hopped by the tigers. Last, a duck walked by them.

_____   _____   _____   _____

D Find the best name for each story. Put the letter of the name on the line.

Names

a. Land and Water Animals
b. The Giant Falls
c. The Giant Wants To Ride
d. Air Is Near Us
e. Air Can Go Fast
f. Animals at the Zoo

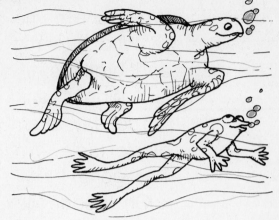

_____ Story 1

Air is all around us. You cannot see it or smell it. But air is there. All plants and animals must have air to live.

_____ Story 2

Frogs and turtles can live in the water. But they can live on land, too. Animals that live on land and in the water can walk and swim. Can ducks and seals do this?

_____ Story 3

Sometimes air moves very fast. It makes a wind. The wind can blow things away. It can make kites fly. The fast air makes sailboats go.

_____ Story 4

Mr. Giant of Pink Lily Pond went to look for a friend. He walked far from the pond. He did not look where he was going. His feet walked right into a tall building. Mr. Giant fell down on top of a big city!

16

On Monday, Helene did not want to eat her cake. She left it on the picnic table and went to play. When she came back, the cake was gone!

"Who took my cake?" said Helene to her sister and brothers.

"I didn't!" said Judy, Mike, and Ben.

Tuesday afternoon, Judy left an orange on the picnic table. When she came back, the orange was gone!

On Wednesday, Mike put bread on the table for lunch. When he went to get more food, someone took the bread.

It happened again on Thursday! Someone took Ben's apple!

Helene wanted to find out who was taking the food. On Friday, she put some candy on the picnic table. Then she hid around the corner of the house. She could not see the table, but

she
could
see
its

Helene saw Judy go by. Then she saw Mike and Ben go by. The candy was still there. Then Helene saw this.

A **Which one is right? Put a** ✔ **by it.**

1. What was this story about?

_____ a. a girl who could think

_____ b. a cat who took food

_____ c. a boy who took food

2. What foods were taken?

_____ a. bread, butter, lettuce, cake

_____ b. eggs, lettuce, orange, candy

_____ c. apple, cake, bread, orange

3. What do we know about the day that Helene hid?

_____ a. It was a hot day.

_____ b. There was no sun that day.

_____ c. The sun was out.

4. Who took the food?

_____ a. a squirrel _____ b. Judy _____ c. Ben

5. Where did Helene hide?

_____ a. under the table in the yard

_____ b. in a tree by the table

_____ c. around the corner of the house

6. When did someone take Ben's apple?

_____ a. Wednesday _____ b. Thursday _____ c. Friday

7. What did Helene see first?

_____ a. her sister and brothers

_____ b. her father and mother

_____ c. a squirrel

8. What is the best name for this story?

_____ a. Mike and the Lost Food

_____ b. Who Took the Food?

_____ c. Ben Takes the Candy

B **Write the name of each thing next to the picture. Then tell which day each thing was taken.**

apple	bread	candy	cake	orange

Thursday	Tuesday	Wednesday	Friday	Monday

	Food	**Day**
1.		
2.		
3.		
4.		
5.		

C What was left on the table? Find a sentence that tells. Put the letter of the sentence by the right table.

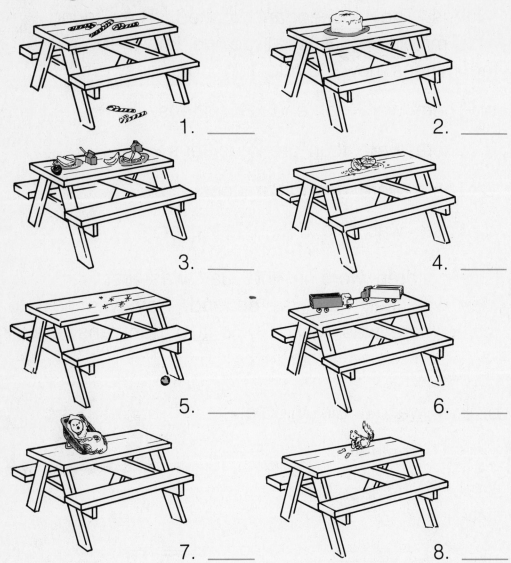

1. _____   2. _____

3. _____   4. _____

5. _____   6. _____

7. _____   8. _____

a. We put a cake on the table to cool.

b. Dad left some coats and hats on the table.

c. Something is here, but the ball rolled off.

d. Some of the candy has fallen on the ground.

e. The squirrel is eating nuts on the table.

f. The baby is not happy on the table alone.

g. The chairs are on top of the table.

h. We left our toy trucks on the table.

i. Our lunch is ready to eat on the table.

j. This orange has many seeds inside.

SKILLS REVIEW (Stories 11–16)

A **Read the stories. Follow the directions.**

1. Tilly, Milly, Billy, and Jilly lost their mittens. They looked and looked. They found nine mittens.  What do we know about the mittens now? Circle <u>two</u> right answers.

   a. There were not enough mittens.

   b. There were four green mittens.

   c. There were enough mittens.

   d. There was one mitten left over.

2. Five children were in line. Jay was first. May was last. Fay was second. Ray was next to last. Where was Kay? Circle <u>two</u> right answers.

   a. Kay was second.

   b. Kay was in the middle.

   c. Kay was third.

   d. Kay was last.

3. Dan got something in the middle store. Nan got something in the first store. Van got something in the last store. Fran got something in the second store. What did the children get? Circle <u>three</u> right answers.

   a. Fran got a book.   b. Jan got some pizza.

   c. Nan got a doll.   d. Van got his hair cut.

B Follow the tiger's tracks. Can you tell where the tiger went? Put a ✔ by the right words.

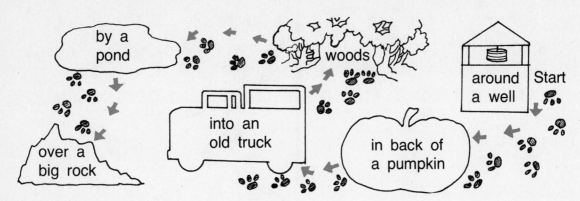

1. Where did the tiger go first?

_____ a. around a well

_____ b. in back of a pumpkin

2. Where did the tiger go last?

_____ a. into the woods

_____ b. over a big rock

3. Where was the tiger before it got to the pond?

_____ a. in the woods

_____ b. at the big rock

4. Where did the tiger go when it left the well?

_____ a. over the water

_____ b. in back of the pumpkin

5. When did the tiger get to the old truck?

_____ a. before it got to the trees

_____ b. after it got to the trees

C Here is a page from a picture dictionary. The words are in ABC order.

banana A banana is long and yellow.

carrot A carrot is long and orange.

doughnut A doughnut is sweet and good to eat.

egg An egg is white or brown.

Write the words from the picture dictionary above.

1. What food sometimes has a hole in the middle?

   _____

   - - - - - - - - - - - - - - - -

   _____

2. What food is picked from trees? _____

   - - - - - - - - - -

3. If you had to put the words **onion** and **fig** on this dictionary page, which word would come first?

   _____

   - - - - - - - - -

   Write the word. _____

4. If you want to put the word **apple** on this page, where would it go? Circle the right answer.

   after **egg**   after **carrot**   before **banana**

78

D Here is the Table of Contents page of a book. Use it to answer the questions. Circle the right answer.

Stories

1. On which page will you find *Care of Your Teeth*?

   a. 10   b. 7   c. 15

2. How many stories are in this book?

   a. 4   b. 5   c. 10

3. Which story starts on page 7?

   a. last one   b. first one   c. middle one

4. Which story is the last one?

   a. *The Pink Candle*

   b. *A Rainy Day*

   c. *The Sticky Mud*

5. Which story is about a light?

   a. *A Worm Tickles Robin*

   b. *Care of Your Teeth*

   c. *The Pink Candle*

E Draw lines to put the first part of the sentence with the last part.

1. A frog's tongue is   a. of tigers.

2. Rain makes   b. the sand wet.

3. We watch T.V. in   c. the baby will cry.

4. Some animals are afraid   d. long and sticky.

5. If you tickle me,   e. I will laugh.

6. Snakes have no   f. the living room.

                                 g. hands and feet.

F Fun time! Guess who? Write the name of the animal next to its picture.

ant   fish   rabbit   seal
snake   squirrel   skunk   tiger

1. _____

2. _____

3. _____

4. _____

5. _____